THE FORMER SOVIET UNION:
THEN AND NOW

The Baltic States:
Then and Now

Adam Woog

ReferencePoint
Press®

© 2015 ReferencePoint Press, Inc.
Printed in the United States

For more information, contact:
ReferencePoint Press, Inc.
PO Box 27779
San Diego, CA 92198
www.ReferencePointPress.com

LIBRARY OF CONGRESS CATALOGING-IN-PUBLICATION DATA

Woog, Adam, 1953-, author.
 The Baltic States: Then and Now/by Adam Woog.
    pages; cm.—(The Former Soviet Union: Then and Now)
 ISBN-13: 978-1-60152-644-1 (hardback)
 ISBN-10: 1-60152-644-X (hardback)
 1. Baltic States—History—20th century. 2. Baltic States—Relations—Soviet Union. 3. Soviet Union—Relations—Baltic States. I. Title. II. Series: Former Soviet Union—then and now.
 DK502.74.W66 2015
 947.908'4—dc23
                                                                    2013040214

☭ CONTENTS

IMPORTANT EVENTS IN THE BALTIC STATES: THEN AND NOW

1924
Josef Stalin becomes the Soviet leader and begins his long reign of dictatorial power.

1945
Following the end of World War II the Soviets are allowed to reoccupy the Baltics, triggering the Cold War between the Soviets and the West.

1920
The Baltic nations declare themselves independent countries in the wake of World War I.

1953
Nikita Khrushchev succeeds Stalin as the USSR's leader, triggering a period of relaxation of oppressive Soviet policies.

1920   **1930**   **1940**   **1950**

1922
The nations under Communist rule, including the Baltics, are amalgamated to become the Union of Soviet Socialist Republic (USSR).

1939
The Molotov-Ribbentrop Pact outlines a plan for dividing the Baltic region between the USSR and Nazi Germany if the Nazis win World War II.

1941
Germany launches an attack on the Baltics, resulting in Nazi occupation until the end of the war.

1949
Operation Priboi becomes the worst single mass deportation of Baltic citizens, sending some ninety thousand people to the gulags, forced labor camps.

1985
Mikhail Gorbachev becomes the Soviet leader and initiates *perestroika* and *glasnost*, reform movements that open the USSR to the West.

2008
The worldwide economic recession slows down the booming Baltic economy.

1990
As the USSR crumbles, the Baltic nations declare their independence.

2011
The Baltic States experience the fastest recovery of all European countries following the 2008 economic crash; Estonia joins the Eurozone.

2013
Lithuania becomes the first Baltic state to head the Council of the European Union, signaling an important milestone in the region's prominence in European politics and economics; Latvia joins the Eurozone.

1990   2000   2010   2020

2014
The Baltic nations confer with their NATO allies over Russia's annexation of Crimea, the autonomous Black Sea republic of southern Ukraine.

2004
The Baltic States join two important organizations allying Western nations, the North Atlantic Treaty Organization and the European Union.

1991
The USSR dissolves, and the rest of its former states follow the Baltics in becoming independent nations.

1989
A huge protest, the Baltic Way, becomes a symbol of the region's growing independence movement.

NATO MEMBER COUNTRIES

ALBANIA   BELGIUM   BULGARIA   CANADA   CROATIA   CZECH REPUBLIC   DENMARK

ESTONIA   FRANCE   GERMANY   GREECE   HUNGARY   ICELAND   ITALY

LATVIA   LITHUANIA   LUXEMBOURG   NETHERLANDS   NORWAY   POLAND   PORTUGAL

ROMANIA   SLOVAKIA   SLOVENIA   SPAIN   TURKEY   UNITED KINGDOM   UNITED STATES

Inside Lithuania, Latvia, and Estonia

By almost any measure, the Baltic States of Lithuania, Latvia, and Estonia are on the rise. Politically, economically, and socially, these nations along the east coast of the Baltic Sea constitute a strong, independent, and thriving region of Europe.

It was not always so. For decades the government of a massive political and economic alliance, the Union of Soviet Socialist Republics (USSR or the Soviet Union), occupied the Baltic States (also known as the Baltics). Throughout most of this period, which began in the early 1940s and ended in the early 1990s, the central Soviet government controlled nearly every aspect of Baltic life, from deciding who could live in certain apartments and have certain jobs to setting wages and monitoring religious worship.

In theory, Soviet rule was supposed to be a boon to the people of the Baltics. Under communism, the Soviet economic and political system, all citizens were to have equal social status, guaranteed jobs, and free education. Everyone would prosper by working together.

But the reality was very different. As with the other regions of the Soviet Union, disastrous economic policies led to chronic shortages of food and other goods. Dissent—that is, any actual or perceived criticism of the Soviet regime—was forbidden, and artistic expression was only allowed if it glorified the state. News of the outside world was suppressed, contact with foreigners was limited, and life was often joyless. Sheila Fitzpatrick, a specialist in Soviet history, paints this impressionistic picture of those years:

The sheer oddness of the way the place functioned [could be seen in] the discomfort and inconvenience, the drabness, the constant shortages and roundabout ways of getting things, the ubiquity of pull and patronage, the insignificance of money, the awfulness of officials. . . . [There was a] sense of being caught in a time warp that was supposed to be the future but felt like the past.[1]

Untold Damage

Citizens of the Baltic States experienced far worse than mere drabness during the Soviet era, especially during the first decades. This was the period of rule by Josef Stalin, the Soviet Union's iron-fisted dictator. Stalin twisted the social and economic ideals of communism to suit his own totalitarian agenda.

Stalin's brutal rule over the Soviet Union is a classic example of totalitarianism. Historian Anne Applebaum comments, "Strictly defined, a totalitarian regime is one that bans all institutions apart from those it has officially approved. A totalitarian regime thus has one political party, one educational system, one artistic creed, one centrally planned economy, one unified media, and one moral code. In a totalitarian state there are no independent schools, no private businesses, no grassroots organizations, and no critical thought."[2]

Stalin's obsession with rooting out dissidents led him to brutally wipe out all signs of anti-Soviet dissent. He once commented, "Ideas are more powerful than guns. We would not let our enemies have guns, why should we let them have ideas?"[3]

Stalin's policies of terror, secrecy, and brutality dominated the Baltics (and the rest of the USSR). Hundreds of thousands of Baltic citizens were exiled to labor camps far from their homes. His unrealistic economic policies created widespread famine, shortages, and death. In short, Stalin's plans were disastrous. A prominent expert on international politics, Anatol

"Ideas are more powerful than guns. We would not let our enemies have guns, why should we let them have ideas?"[3]

—Soviet dictator Josef Stalin.

Lieven, comments, "It is difficult to exaggerate the amount of damage done to the Baltic States by Soviet rule."[4]

Freedom

After Stalin's death in 1953, the Soviets dropped the worst of the dictator's policies, such as the imprisonment or execution of political dissidents, but it continued to tightly control life in the Baltics. Citizens still could not freely express their ideas. Nor could they openly worship as they pleased. But that changed dramatically in the late 1980s when anti-Soviet demonstrations—beginning in the Baltics and spreading to the rest of the Soviet-dominated nations—forced the central Moscow-led government to enact a series of reforms. These reforms, known as *glasnost* and *perestroika*, contributed to the eventual collapse of the Soviet Union and ultimately to independence for Lithuania, Latvia, and Estonia.

Events leading to this point moved much faster than anyone, including citizens of the Baltics, had ever envisioned. Archie Brown, a British professor of political science, comments, "The speed with which the Soviet system was transformed and the Soviet state disintegrated took almost everyone by surprise. . . . Even the most disaffected nationalities in the Soviet Union—a description that fitted the Baltic peoples of Estonia, Latvia and Lithuania—did not in their wildest dreams believe [that they would soon] be living in independent states."[5]

A Time of Growth

The decades since independence have been an exhilarating time of growth, economically and socially. For example, when taken together the Baltics have one of Europe's best economic growth rates. And individuals in the Baltics are now free to do many things that were previously denied them. They can freely express themselves politically and artistically; if they have the means, they can travel abroad; and those with entrepreneurial spirit and know-how can start and run their own businesses.

For example, Jurgis and Danute Zabaliunas are two of the many Baltic citizens who now operate their own business—a bed and breakfast in the city of Kaunas in Lithuania. Before independence in 1991, a business such as this one would have been impossible to imagine. Foreigners would never have been allowed to stay in the homes of ordinary Lithuanians. Jurgis comments, "Things are much better now. I can vote,

I am not afraid to speak and for creative types there are many more possibilities. Life is good."[6]

This "good life" for the people of the Baltics today encompasses political, personal, economic, and social freedoms. These are concepts that were almost unthinkable for a long time—hundreds of years, in fact, long before the advent of the Soviet era.

CHAPTER ONE

Controlling the Baltics

The period in which foreign nations occupied the Baltics stretches back centuries. During this long era, the native peoples of the Baltics were little more than pawns in wars fought by foreign rulers who sought control of the region's valuable seaports. The nation that controlled the ports could move people, goods, and military supplies wherever they were needed most, especially in the vast region between Europe and Russia.

So it was nothing new when the Soviet Union occupied the region beginning in the 1920s. Other countries had done the same for a long time, sometimes to devastating effect. Historian Andrejs Plakans comments, "The political history of the [Baltics] contains far more discontinuity than years of peace, many more regime changes than periods of stable governance, and much more destruction than uninterrupted growth."[7]

Swedish and Russian Occupation

In the late seventeenth and early eighteenth centuries, the Baltics were part of what was then the Swedish Empire, which also included what are now Sweden, Finland, Norway, and portions of, among other nations, Denmark, Poland, and Germany. But the Swedish Empire's control of the Baltics did not last. It began to falter in the early eighteenth century, in large part because Sweden was weakened by its involvement in war elsewhere. Another large dominion, the Russian Empire, was able to take advantage of this weakness.

The Russian Empire stretched the vast distance from the Baltic Sea east to what is today Alaska. The Russian czar at the time, Peter the Great, succeeded in incorporating the Baltics into this territory by the late 1720s. For the next two centuries, Peter's successors controlled almost all the region around the Baltic Sea, including what are today Lithuania, Estonia, Latvia, and to the north, Finland.

During the next two centuries, the Russians imposed their own ways on traditional life in each of the Baltic countries. Some of these impositions were oppressive. For example, Russian became the official language of all three countries; use of the Latvian, Lithuanian, and Estonian languages was banned. But other changes were positive. Notably, the new rulers outlawed serfdom, a practice that was common across Europe in medieval times but continued in all of the Baltic States well past the Middle Ages. Serfs were peasants who lived on and worked land owned by nobles; they were beholden to the landowner and therefore obligated to provide labor, subject to fees and fines, and under jurisdiction of the noble's courts. Over the centuries of Russian domination, the people of the Baltics resisted as much as possible. They lacked the resources to oppose Russia's military might, but they were able to resist in small ways. For example, throughout the Baltics people boycotted books printed in Russian. Instead, books in native languages were secretly printed and smuggled across borders. Another example was the system called "schools of the hearth," essentially informal home-schooling organizations that villages created as alternatives to the official Russian educational system.

The Bolshevik Revolution

The Russian Empire ended with a cataclysmic event: the Bolshevik Revolution of 1917. This uprising toppled the royal family and replaced it with a political and economic system called communism. (*Bolshevik* referred to one faction of the Communist Party that overthrew the czar.)

The Communists abolished distinctions between social classes, forcing people to refer to each other simply as "comrade." They also replaced open elections with a single-party system of government and replaced private ownership with collective ownership. Theoretically, that meant that the citizens of a Communist country controlled all means of production (such as farms and factories) and distribution (such as railroads). In practice, however, this simply meant government control.

By overthrowing the royal family and theoretically handing control of the country to the people, the Bolsheviks drastically changed the shape of Russian life. At the same time, another cataclysmic event also had a dramatic impact on the Baltics. This was World War I (1914–1918), which pitted Germany against a group of nations led by the United Kingdom, France, the United States, and (until the revolution toppled it) the Russian Empire.

The Baltic States were caught in the middle of the war's chaos, and the situation became more complicated when the Bolsheviks took control of Russia. One important aspect of the Bolshevik plan was to export Communist ideals to other countries, by force if necessary. Essentially, the Bolsheviks sought to occupy and dominate as many nations as possible. They succeeded in many cases, and in 1922 several once-independent countries were amalgamated into the Union of Soviet Socialist Republics. (*Soviet* refers to political councils or assemblies.)

The Bolshevik Revolution of 1917 (pictured) toppled the Russian monarchy and brought to power a new regime, which adhered to Communist doctrine. The neighboring Baltic States of Latvia, Lithuania, and Estonia were caught in the middle of this cataclysmic change.

Latvian Fighters

Documents from the archives of the Hoover Institution at Stanford University describe Latvian involvement in the Russian Revolution and civil war.

Latvians participated in large numbers in the convulsions of the Russian Revolution and ensuing civil war. . . . After the 1917 revolution, detachments of Latvian riflemen, or *strelnieki* . . . became legendary for their exploits, both on behalf of the Bolsheviks and against them in the service of White armies. . . . By the end of the Russian civil war, many riflemen had returned to Latvia, disillusioned with the increasingly authoritarian character of Bolshevism. These played a part in securing Latvian independence. Those Latvians who continued to support the Bolsheviks remained in Russia; many later lost their lives in the Stalinist purges of the 1930s.

Hoover Institution, "Baltic States 1918–1938," Libraries and Archives, Stanford University. www.hoover.org.

A Brief Period of Independence

The Bolsheviks aimed to include the Baltics as well. However, there was a brief period of independence for the region before this came about. For roughly two decades after World War I, the Baltics enjoyed an unfamiliar status: freedom. Estonia, Latvia, and Lithuania had been part of an empire that no longer existed—and the Bolsheviks were not yet ready to occupy them. So the three Baltic countries declared independence and in 1920 were formally recognized as such by the other nations of the world.

The following two decades of independence were exciting and heady times for the people of Latvia, Lithuania, and Estonia. They held open elections to appoint politicians who were eager to strengthen their place in the world and took several important steps to ensure this. For example, they knew that a Bolshevik invasion was a distinct possibility, so they negotiated peace treaties with Russia that were designed to prevent such an event. As a result Estonia's treaty assured its independence and established a firm border between the two countries. In return, Russia was given the ability to create a port and a power station in Estonia. The new republics also drafted constitutions ensuring reforms such as voting rights for women and the creation of elected parliaments. And the Baltics bolstered their respective economies by signing trade agreements with several key Western countries.

But the Baltic States' newfound status was always shaky, and within a few years it failed. There were several reasons for this. For one thing, a worldwide economic depression in 1929 (known as the Great Depression) hit the poor, small Baltic region hard and crippled its economic base. But there was another, even more devastating reason—the rise to power of Germany's Nazi Party.

The leader of the Nazis, Adolf Hitler, had grandiose plans to conquer all of Europe and beyond. As Germany overran parts of Europe and headed toward open war, other nations banded together to oppose the threat. These nations, led by the United Kingdom and France, became known as the Allies. (The United States did not formally join the war until 1941.)

The situation grew steadily more precarious as Hitler grew bolder. In 1938 Germany annexed Austria, and in 1939 the Nazis invaded and occupied Poland. This triggered World War II, the bloodiest conflict in history.

The Secret Protocol

As before, the Baltic region was an important prize. Because it lay between Germany and the USSR, it was coveted by both Hitler and Josef Stalin, who had been the Soviet Union's leader since 1924.

At first, Stalin had avoided aligning himself with either the Nazis or the Allies. But he also feared an invasion by Germany, and so he joined forces with the Allies. At the same time, Stalin shrewdly arranged a fragile peace agreement with Germany. Specifically, in 1939 Germany and the USSR signed a document called the Molotov-Ribbentrop Pact. In it the two nations agreed that for ten years they would not invade each other's land.

But the Molotov-Ribbentrop Pact was more than just a peace agreement. It also contained a secret section called, in diplomatic terms, a protocol. This secret protocol would soon have consequences for the Baltics serious enough to change the course of history. This secret protocol outlined a way to carve up much of Europe, including the Baltics, if the Nazis won the war. The Germans and the Soviets agreed that they would divide Northern and Eastern Europe between them, creating two "spheres of influence." Under these terms, most of the Baltic region would become part of the Soviet Union.

The Occupation Begins

As the war raged, Stalin moved his Red Army, so called for the symbolic color of communism, west toward the Baltic nations. Although he stopped short of outright invasion, throughout 1939 and 1940 Stalin ordered increasingly aggressive military action there. For example, he ordered Soviet warships to anchor off Baltic ports and Soviet bombers to fly over the capital cities of the Baltic nations. The Red Army also raided military posts along borders. As the situation escalated, the Soviets grew bolder, demanding that their army be allowed to establish its own military bases there.

> "Fully understanding the futility of military resistance, the Baltic leaders had no choice but to accept the USSR's ultimatums."[8]
>
> —Historian Kevin O'Connor.

Faced with a far larger force than they could fight and wanting to avoid open war, the governments of the Baltic countries yielded in 1940. In practical terms, it seemed the only option. Historian Kevin O'Connor writes, "Fully understanding the futility of military resistance, the Baltic leaders had no choice but to accept the USSR's ultimatums."[8]

Not surprisingly, the majority of Baltic citizens did not welcome the Russians. They had no desire to give up their freedom. When full-scale resistance proved impossible, ordinary citizens formed pockets of armed resistance and carried out guerrilla warfare—that is, small-scale attacks such as raiding military posts in search of weapons.

Chief among the resistance fighters were thousands of men and women called the Forest Brothers, so named because they hid out in the region's timbered hills and farmland. The bands of Forest Brothers ranged in size from eight hundred individuals down to handfuls who hid out in bunkers or underneath houses and farm buildings. They generally moved from place to place, never spending more than a few weeks in one spot. The Forest Brothers were thus able to escape almost certain arrest and imprisonment. One such rebel was Estonian Alfred Kaarman, whose brother was arrested and sent to a prison camp. In 2003, aged eighty-one, Kaarman recalled, "'I didn't want that to happen to me. We understood that it is better to die in the forest with a weapon in your hands than in a Soviet camp.'"[9]

The New Governments

Once the Baltic governments gave in to the Soviets in 1940, Stalin began the transformation of his newly acquired land into Soviet states. This meant changing virtually all aspects of life to fit the Soviet model, ranging from

An armored column of Nazi troops streams into Poland in 1939, igniting World War II in Europe. The start of war led to an agreement between Germany and the Soviet Union—including a pact that determined who would control the Baltic States.

The Struggle for Self-Determination

In one form or another, dissidents have always spoken out in favor of Baltic independence. It is a process that has been going on for hundreds of years, from earlier centuries through the region's brief period of independence in the 1920s and 1930s, and on to today's independent status. Journalist Anatol Lieven comments, "The Baltic independence movement of our own time can be seen as part of a continuous, closely-linked struggle for national self-determination and cultural identity which began under Russian imperial rule in the nineteenth century, and within which the independent states [of the 1920s and 1930s] were only an interlude, albeit an immensely important one."

Anatol Lieven, *The Baltic Revolution: Estonia, Latvia, Lithuania and the Path to Independence.* New Haven, CT: Yale University Press, 1993, p. xiv.

large changes, such as sweeping economic reforms, to smaller changes, such as making Russian once again the only official language. Plakans writes, "Sovietization proceeded apace in all domains of life in each country."[10] With the new governments came new names: the Estonian Soviet Socialist Republic, the Latvian Soviet Socialist Republic, and the Lithuanian Soviet Socialist Republic.

Each of these new "republics" had a puppet government that followed the Communist Party line and answered to Moscow. Elections were held in each country in 1940 to appoint these new officials. But only pro-Communist candidates appeared on the ballots. Despite the obvious outcome of the elections, the Soviets used veiled threats to enforce maximum turnout at the polls. For example, on the first day of elections in June 1940, Estonia's main daily newspaper warned: "It would be extremely unwise to shirk elections. . . . Only [the] people's enemies stay at home on election day."[11]

Frightened of possible punishment, most of the Baltic population went to the polls and voted the pro-Soviet candidates into office. Some of these newly elected officials were natives of the Baltics who were also reliably pro-Soviet. On the other hand, many newly elected politicians were not native. Instead, they were ethnic Russians—loyal Communist Party members brought in from farther east in the USSR. In any case officials sought to convince the Baltic people that the Soviet regimes would be benevolent and positive, there only to provide guidance and protection. One such official was Lithuania's new minister of the interior, Mečislovas Gedvilas, who stated, "The essential fundamentals of our country have not been changed. No one threatens rightful private property or wealth. The Red Army came to our country not to change our way of life, but only to protect us from the dangers of war and to help us maintain our independence."[12]

The Spoils of War

Once the new governments were in place, the Stalinist regime began the next phase of its plan: restructuring the Baltics to fit the Soviet mold. But before this process of Sovietization could be completed, another cataclysmic event took place. In the summer of 1941, Germany broke its nonaggression promise and launched a successful attack on the Baltics.

At first, some citizens of the region welcomed the Nazis. They saw the German invaders as the lesser of two evils—potential liberators who might be better than the oppressive Soviet puppet governments. Historian Prit Buttar writes, "As the Germans marched into Lithuania, they were greeted by jubilant crowds and thousands of people who threw bunches of flowers to the men they regarded as saviours from the Bolsheviks."[13]

"It would be extremely unwise to shirk elections. Only [the] people's enemies stay at home on election day."[11]

—Estonia's main daily newspaper

But these hopes soon evaporated as the Nazis established their own governments in each country and began carrying out their horrific programs—most of all, the extermination of Jews and other minority groups. The Germans continued to occupy the Baltics, sending Jews to concentration camps and enacting other repressive policies, until the end of the war in 1945.

At this point, Baltic history took another major turn. The Allied forces had beaten the Germans, and in the wake of their victory they chose to turn a blind eye toward the future of Latvia, Estonia, and Lithuania. Specifically, the Allies did not stop the plans of their World War II ally, Josef Stalin. The Red Army had been a major force in defeating the Nazis, so as a reward for being on the side of the winners, the Allies reluctantly allowed Stalin to claim the Baltics for a second time. Winston Churchill, the British prime minister, commented, "We accept that the Soviet claims for . . . disputed territory such as the Baltic States are wrong—they are unjust—but there is no practical method of putting this right."[14]

The Postwar Occupation Begins

The Stalinist regime quickly moved its troops and government officials back into the Baltics. These new Soviet-backed authorities, as had happened earlier, tried to reassure the region's citizens that they would be in good hands. So some inhabitants chose to stay, despite misgivings about the new regime. Plakans comments, "The three governments sought in all ways possible to portray the overall situation as normal. . . . The general public went along with it; rumors swirled, but most people continued with the routines of daily life."[15]

On the other hand, tens of thousands of Baltic residents fled the region, hoping to find sanctuary in Sweden, Finland, or other countries. And as Stalin moved his military and government forces back into the region, he could not resist gloating over his reclaimed land. He stated in 1945, "The Baltic coast—Russian land for centuries—is ours again."[16] And so the long era of postwar Soviet occupation began.

CHAPTER TWO

Politics in the Baltics

The Soviet Union's absorption of the Baltic nations brought sweeping changes to the region's political systems. Before occupation, during their period of prewar independence, the Baltics had been able to establish freely elected governments and enact political reforms such as voting rights for women. But when the Soviets invaded, existing laws and political structures were dissolved and previously elected politicians forced out.

One was Lithuania's president, Antanas Smetona. Smetona had initially proposed armed resistance against the Soviets, but most of the country's leaders rejected the idea, knowing that they could not realistically battle the Red Army. Unable to put his plan into action, Smetona resigned and fled the country. His counterparts in the other Baltic nations, Konstantin Päts of Estonia and Karlis Ulmanis of Latvia, briefly remained in office, until Soviet authorities forced them to resign. The two were later unjustly convicted of anti-Soviet sabotage and imprisoned.

All of the former Baltic leaders and their administrations were replaced by "people's governments." (This was a phrase commonly used by the Stalinist regime to describe the Communist ideal of a nation's government controlled by its citizens.) Along with these new administrations, the nations were given new names that suggested they retained independent identities as Soviet Socialist Republics. But these new countries were independent republics in name only.

Administrative Structure

The new nations' administrations were structured in a similar way to the overall Soviet model. Each nation had a major body of legislators, the Supreme Soviet, that was elected every four years. (*Soviet* in this case referred to a council for each country, not the USSR as a whole).

Ostensibly, the citizens of the Baltics elected the members of their respective Supreme Soviets. But—as with the elections Stalin had held when the Soviets first occupied the region—they were essentially meaningless. There was still only one slate of candidates—those of the Communist Party.

Furthermore, the Supreme Soviets of the Baltic countries had little real power. They met only twice a year, for a few days each time. The real power in each case was held by the Presidium, a permanent body of about sixteen lawmakers. This body had, among other powers, the ability to appoint officials in the executive branch of the government, and the chair of the Presidium was in essence the head of state. In all of the Baltic nations, laws were made unanimously and with little debate—making the Supreme Soviet and Presidium essentially "rubber-stamp" entities that simply approved directives from Moscow.

The Nomenklatura

On a regional and local level, a large bureaucracy, the *nomenklatura*, administered laws and regulations. It was not officially necessary for someone to be a member of the Communist Party in order to be employed in the nomenklatura. However, virtually everyone who wanted to work within the system found it beneficial to belong.

Government jobs were desirable because they brought with them special privileges and benefits such as a car, a better apartment, or access to good food. So Baltic citizens had a strong incentive to join the party and curry favor with those who could give them jobs or help them rise within the system.

In keeping with the Communist tenet of equality, the governmental bodies of each country included some representatives of their respective ethnic groups (native Estonians in Estonia, for example). However, these

Two men read the official Communist Party newspaper Pravda. *Under Soviet control, news in the Baltics—and all other Soviet-controlled states—was tightly restricted.*

native ethnic groups were dramatically underrepresented, and those who were part of the process were loyal party members. The majority of "elected" officials and members of the nomenklatura were nonnatives brought in from farther east in the USSR who could be relied on to follow Moscow's policies. These "imported" lawmakers were typically ethnic Russians and had little knowledge of or interest in local customs.

A Ban on Foreign News

Until Stalin's death in 1953, the Baltic people had no chance to protest this rigid and closed political situation. Any kind of dissent, in fact, risked severe punishment. So they found ways to protest in small, personal ways. Pretending not to understand Russian, placing flowers on the graves of Baltic national heroes, using national colors for decorations, cheering for national sports teams playing against Russians—all of these were minor but pointed insults.

The Forest Brothers

An estimated fifty thousand guerrilla fighters—the Forest Brothers, so called for their hiding places—battled Soviet occupation of their lands. Roughly forty thousand of these fighters were in Lithuania, with the rest in Estonia and Latvia. Although the movement eventually died out, many Forest Brothers hated the Soviets so much that they stayed in hiding well into the 1950s. Historian Andrejs Plakans comments:

> They were well armed, having brought weapons along from their former military units, and they successfully raided Soviet armories. Referred to generically as "bandits" by Soviet authorities, the forest brothers harassed Soviet functionaries, especially in rural areas; fought pitched battles against the search-and-destroy military units sent to flush them out of their hideouts; and requisitioned or stole food however they could.

Andrejs Plakans, *A Concise History of the Baltic States*. Cambridge: Cambridge University Press, 2011, pp. 360–62.

Another aspect of the political environment in the Baltics was the Soviet ban on foreign news outlets. Meanwhile, the government controlled the only available media outlets (such as the official Communist Party newspaper, *Pravda*, and a few state-run TV and radio stations). The lack of foreign news kept people in the region from learning about politics (and other aspects of life) in the outside world, so Baltic citizens knew only what the Soviets wanted them to learn.

The Khrushchev Thaw

Such censorship was part of an overall atmosphere of distrust between the Soviet Union and the nations of the West—especially the United States. This tense period, characterized by espionage and arms buildup on both sides, was called the Cold War. Unlike a formal "hot" war, it never erupted into outright battle between the two primary foes (the USSR and the United States); rather, they armed allies and fought wars on behalf of those who opposed the influences of one side or the other. The Cold War strongly affected the Baltics, notably in the region's role as a major location for missile sites, naval and air bases, radio stations, and other military operations.

However, the Cold War sometimes "thawed." This was because Nikita Khrushchev, who had emerged as Stalin's successor after the dictator's death in 1953, reversed the worst of Stalin's repressive programs, especially those affecting human rights. The most important development was the closure of the *gulags*, Stalin's forced labor camps. By 1956 the last of these camps had closed, and their remaining prisoners—including thousands of people from the Baltics—regained their freedom. Other changes included the stoppage of routine jamming of foreign radio and TV broadcasts, which were aimed specifically at the Baltic region because of its proximity to the West. When the jamming stopped, Baltic citizens could receive a certain amount of foreign news and commentary for the first time in years.

Stepping Stones

The ability to receive at least a certain amount of news and commentary from the outside world had a strong impact on people in the Baltics who were critical of the government. For example, in the 1970s dissidents there began hearing about protest movements in the West against the Vietnam War and other issues. Learning about these protests encouraged them to begin speaking out more openly, although they still risked retaliation.

Underground pro-nationalist organizations had always been present in the Baltics, even during the worst years of Soviet repression. Activists were able to protest more openly in the 1970s, but they still had to be careful not to criticize the government too overtly. Frequently, they used less controversial issues, such as artistic freedom, as stepping stones to more open political criticism.

One example of this revolved around *The Chronicle of the Catholic Church in Lithuania*, an underground journal that first appeared in 1972. Officially, it was dedicated to defending religious freedom. But direct support of religious freedom by extension meant indirect support of political freedom. Historian Tonu Parming, writing in 1977, commented, "In Lithuania, religious issues evoke strong nationality responses, and religion is often used as a channel for expressing what essentially amounts to nationalist dissent."[17]

Support and Inspiration

These activists were further inspired by words of support from Western leaders. Specifically, they learned that Western politicians were reasserting their opinion that the Soviet occupation of the Baltics was illegal. This had been a major point of disagreement for years between the USSR and the West.

The Soviet Union had always insisted that the Baltic nations had voluntarily invited it in and that the Soviets were there only for the benefit of the Baltic people. The USSR's presence there was thus legitimate under international law. Typical of this sentiment was a 1960 editorial in the official Latvian Communist Party journal, which commented, "One should explain the force that stands behind the friendship of nations, the extent of the assistance rendered by the brotherly Soviet republics, and principally by the trusted friend of the Latvians—the Russian nation—in reconstructing the Latvian economy and culture."[18]

A significant shift in this ongoing situation was an event in 1975: the signing by the United States, Canada, and nearly all of the European nations of a document called the Helsinki Accords. In this document the nations of the West reasserted their position that the Soviet Union was illegally occupying Latvia, Estonia, and Lithuania.

On the Forefront of the Protest Movement

By the mid-1980s protests were woven into the fabric of daily life in the Baltics. Olgerts Eglitis, a Latvian activist during that period, comments, "On June 14th 1987 . . . news about an unsanctioned anti-Soviet demonstration in Latvia's capital spread in the Western media. After that the country never came to rest: the spell of fear and subjugation evaporated, and mass demonstrations, protest meetings, and acts of civil disobedience became part of daily life in Latvia."[19]

But the Baltics were by no means the only Soviet-dominated nations to foster a growing pro-independence protest movement. Similar efforts were taking place elsewhere in the USSR. Nonetheless, Latvia, Lithuania, and Estonia were on the movement's leading edge, in large part because of the region's exposure to outside TV and radio and the encouragement provided by the Helsinki Accords.

The extent of the Baltics' leadership role can be seen in the fact that from the early to mid-1970s, nearly 20 percent of all nationalist protests in the USSR occurred in the Baltic States. Since the region contained less than 2 percent of the total population, the number of protests, measured on a per-capita basis, was far higher than in other Soviet-controlled nations.

Indirect Protests

Pro-independence activists in the Baltics were successful in gaining momentum for their cause, in part because they employed methods that did not openly criticize the government. For example, in many cases they formed organizations devoted to causes such as the environment or the revival of regional languages. These organizations served as ways to indirectly criticize the government and its practices during a period when open debate was still dangerous.

One example of a stand-in for outright dissent was the environmental movement, which focused on issues that were a major concern for activists in the West as well. Protest against environmental dangers such as nuclear waste served as training grounds for more overt political protests that came later. Inesis Kiskis, now a top environmental official in Lithuania, recalls, "The environment was . . . a neutral issue, and it was new. In Lithuania, environmental consciousness preceded independence."[20]

> "The environment was . . . a neutral issue, and it was new. In Lithuania, environmental consciousness preceded independence."[20]
>
> —Lithuanian environmental activist Inesis Kiskis.

As the independence movement in the Baltics gained momentum, the region's authorities were forced to allow more and more reforms. A watershed moment came in 1985, when a new Soviet leader, Mikhail Gorbachev, rose to power. Gorbachev was a reformer who hoped to foster close political relations with the Western nations by launching two related policies: *glasnost* ("openness") and *perestroika* ("restructuring"). These policies included reforms such as greater free speech, open democratic elections, and the creation of semiprivate businesses in place of governmental ownership.

Glasnost and Perestroika Take Hold

The citizens of the Baltics closely followed Gorbachev's reforms. One aspect of the reforms was that for the first time, the people of the Baltics were able to watch live, uncensored coverage on TV of debates in the legislature. Such access to the workings of government was nothing new in the West, but in the Baltics it was exciting and amazing. In some parts of the region, agricultural and industrial production ground to a halt as millions of workers abandoned their jobs to watch TV coverage of their government in action.

"New revelations filled the newspapers every day, a dizzying array of institutional changes were enacted and dozens (at times hundreds) of protests were mounted daily [in the USSR]."[21]

—Political scientist Mark R. Beissinger.

Furthermore, for the first time since the beginning of the Soviet occupation, political organizations other than the Communist Party were allowed to take part in elections. A major victory was scored in 1988 when elections were held for the Congress of People's Deputies, the highest governing authority for the entire Soviet Union. The results were dramatic: pro-independence candidates won landslide victories in all three countries, such as capturing thirty-six out of Lithuania's forty seats.

The pro-independence movement in the Baltics continued to pick up speed and intensity in the late 1980s. Political scientist Mark R. Beissinger comments, "New revelations filled the newspapers every day, a dizzying array of institutional changes were enacted and dozens (at times hundreds) of protests were mounted daily [in the USSR]—many of them spectacular events."[21]

The Singing Revolution

Many of these "spectacular events" reflected an unusual feature of dissent in the Baltics. Coming from the region's long history of public singing and large-scale song festivals, group singing became a key part of the protest movement. Large gatherings of protestors would regularly meet in town squares and other public places to perform officially outlawed songs, such as religious hymns and national anthems. Singing became such a prominent feature of every demonstration, in fact, that the Baltics' pro-independence movement has been called the Singing Revolution.

The Iron Curtain

When Lithuania, Latvia, and Estonia came under Soviet control, they became part of a bloc of nations known as the Iron Curtain countries. These were countries that existed, in essence, behind a barrier separating Soviet-controlled territory from the Western world. The phrase was coined in 1946 by Winston Churchill, who had been the British prime minister during World War II, when he stated: "From Stettin in the Baltic to Trieste in the Adriatic an iron curtain has descended across the Continent."

As part of this bloc, the Baltics played a part in a tense impasse that existed between the West and the USSR. Notably, the Red Army used the region as a major location for missile sites, numerous naval and air bases, radio stations, and other military operations.

Quoted in *Modern History Sourcebook*, "Winston S. Churchill: 'Iron Curtain Speech,' March 5, 1946," Fordham University. www.fordham.edu.

The single most astonishing protest of this period was an event, the Baltic Way, that involved 1 to 2 million people (estimates vary). It occurred on August 23, 1989—the fiftieth anniversary of the signing of the Molotov-Ribbentrop Pact, the agreement between Russia and Germany that had been key to the Soviet occupation. The enormous number of people who turned out formed a human chain that stretched for more than 400 miles (644 km), passing through the capitals of all three Baltic countries.

The Baltic Way was a dramatic demonstration of the feeling shared by activists and ordinary people that they would no longer accept Soviet domination. Their hopeful attitude was symbolized by the tearful comments of Janis Blum, a Latvian engineer, as he attended a May 1989 rally where a crowd of thousands sang the national anthem, "God Bless Latvia." A *New York Times* article quoted Blum: "The last time I sang this song freely was the 18th of July 1940. My dream is to once again sing it as a completely free man."[22]

In the spring of 1990 Blum was able to fulfill that dream, when his country, as well as Lithuania and Estonia, declared independence. Immediately after these declarations, it seemed likely that the Soviets would retaliate with violence. Aggression and punishment had almost always been the response to anti-Soviet protests, and there were indeed a few violent incidents. For example, early in 1991 Lithuanian activists occupied a television tower in the capital city of Vilnius. Fourteen of the protestors were killed when Soviet troops tried to reclaim the facility. A young protestor, Jolita Maslunita, told a reporter that, in her opinion, Moscow had made the TV tower a primary target because it was Lithuania's primary connection with the world. Maslunita added that the protestors remained determined despite the deaths. She commented, "We are not afraid, even now. . . . We must have our own free Lithuania, even though we could all be wounded."[23]

> "We are not afraid, even now. . . . We must have our own free Lithuania, even though we could all be wounded."[23]
>
> —Lithuanian activist Jolita Maslunita.

New and Untried Systems

The failed attempt by the Soviets to reclaim the TV tower in Vilnius illustrated the once powerful empire's inability to stop the independence movement, and throughout 1991 the USSR continued to crumble. The end came with its formal dissolution late that year. In its place were a number of new entities, including the three Baltic nations. Several of these new nations, including Russia, Belarus, and Ukraine, formed a loose affiliation called the Commonwealth of Independent States. It was all that remained of the Soviet empire.

The end of Soviet communism was an exhilarating period for the people of the Baltics. For them, freedom—almost unthinkable for a very long time—was now a reality. Lievan comments, "For more than four decades, it seemed that the independent Baltic states and cultures [were] doomed irretrievably to be submerged within the Soviet Union, and remembered only by groups of Baltic émigrés forever separated from their homelands by the Iron Curtain."[24]

Now everything was different. But the joy of newfound freedom in the Baltics was tempered by the knowledge that there was work to be done. For four decades the region had been part of a huge, centrally controlled

Bearing flowers, Lithuanian women mourn the activists killed by Soviet troops during an altercation at a Vilnius television tower in 1991. The activists sought Lithuania's independence from Soviet control.

empire. Now the Republics of Lithuania, Estonia, and Latvia (as the countries were renamed) had to create completely new political, economic, and social structures. For example, extensive services were needed to help families and individuals support themselves, since Moscow no longer took care of such aspects of daily life as health care. Andrejs Plakans comments:

> The human side of the transition proved to be wrenching in the extreme. For five decades, the populations of the three new republics had grown accustomed to a Soviet-style welfare state in which most social services were available without cost, and monies for a host of different purposes, including pensions, came from a centralized state budget. . . . The old system had engendered dependency; now, each citizen was to be responsible for his or her own personal income, career path, savings, competitive sense, and ultimate survival.[25]

The creation of new political structures required a series of daunting tasks, including dismantling the old Soviet-style bureaucracy in favor of Western-style government. This major step signaled the desire of Baltic officials to distance themselves from the memory of Soviet rule by forming an alliance with the democratic West. O'Connor comments, "Their destiny, they concurred, was with the West."[26]

And so the old system was replaced with constitutions and democratic parliamentary governments modeled on those of Western nations. In each of the Baltic nations, citizens have (among other privileges) the right to vote for a true slate of candidates. This democratic system symbolizes the dramatic changes in the Baltics' overall political structure in the years since independence, and it continues to serve them well.

CHAPTER THREE

Economics in the Baltics

The economic life of the Baltics underwent a fundamental transformation during the years of Soviet occupation. Previously, the Baltic nations, although poor compared to the more developed countries of the West, had operated under a free-market (capitalist) system. That economic system changed radically when the USSR took control. For one thing, the Russian ruble became the official currency, replacing the established Estonian, Latvian, and Lithuanian currencies. More significantly, the Soviets imposed the sweeping economic policies of communism.

Communism was supposed to help the Baltics increase production of food and manufactured goods. However, a combination of factors—notably Stalin's brutal methods of enforcement—caused this scheme to fail and led to decades of misery, deprivation, and in some cases death.

Collectivizing the Farms

The Baltic nations were mostly rural, and agriculture and related industries had been the cornerstone of the region's economy for centuries. Each nation had particular strengths. For example, Lithuania was especially known for livestock such as pigs, Estonia for potatoes and grain, and Latvia for its dairy products. Most farms were small and family-owned. In many ways the farm life of the Baltics had not changed significantly for centuries. The work was mostly done by hand, using workhorses and primitive tools.

The advent of communism destroyed many of the old ways of Baltic agriculture. Notably, communism's principle of social equality, in economic terms, meant eliminating private ownership. In its place was group ownership and operation of farms. One key aspect of this development was that Baltic farmers were forced to consolidate their land into huge, communal farms. This process was called collectivization. Stalin's theory was that collectivized farms would modernize and improve the primitive state of Baltic agriculture. In so doing, Stalin asserted, the region would produce enough food—especially grain for bread—to export to other parts of the Soviet Union. In 1928 he stated, "Agriculture is developing slowly, comrades. This is because we have about 25 million individually owned farms [throughout the USSR]. They are the most primitive and undeveloped form of economy. We must do our utmost to develop large farms and to convert them into grain factories for the country, organised on a modem scientific basis."[27]

> "We are 50 to 100 years behind the advanced countries. We must cover this distance in 10 years. Either we do this or they will crush us."[28]
>
> —Soviet dictator Josef Stalin, 1931.

Creating Heavy Industry

Besides agriculture, a second mainstay of the Baltic economy had been light manufacturing. As with agriculture, each country had particular strengths. For example, Latvia was known for paper products, Estonia for small electronics such as radios, and Lithuania for clothing and textiles. Like the region's farms, these businesses were also nationalized.

Stalin's plan for the Baltic nations replaced much of its light industry (and some of its agricultural land) with heavy manufacturing factories such as those for steelmaking, shipbuilding, and chemical production. In large part these changes were made because Stalin was fanatically concerned with quickly bringing the Soviet Union's industrial capabilities to the level of the West's. In 1931 he remarked, "We are 50 to 100 years behind the advanced countries. We must cover this distance in 10 years. Either we do this or they will crush us."[28]

Building new factories for heavy industry was a formidable task under any circumstances. But it was especially so in the Baltics during the mid- to late 1940s, in the aftermath of World War II. The conflict had damaged or obliterated many of the region's existing factories. Some were destroyed during battle, whereas others were deliberately demolished to keep them from enemy hands. Much of the Baltics' infrastructure, such as roads and

The Baltic economies relied heavily on agriculture before the Soviet program of collectivization began. Most farming involved small, family-owned farms where work was done by hand, as can be seen in this photograph of a woman milking her cow in Estonia.

water systems, was also in ruins. As a result, Prit Buttar notes, "The war had a huge impact on the economies of the three countries."[29]

The Five-Year Plans

The sweeping changes in the Baltics' agricultural and manufacturing sectors were part of an ambitious series of Five-Year Plans ordered by Stalin. They were designed to reach ever-higher production goals and in time make the USSR self-sufficient. At first it appeared that the early Five-Year Plans might succeed. Production rates improved—an impressive feat considering that during this period the rest of the world was suffering from the massive economic crisis known as the Great Depression. However, Stalin's plans had grievous flaws. Among them was the fact that replacement parts for industrial machinery were scarce, and factories were often forced to shut for long periods before the parts could be found or made. Also, a lack of skilled factory workers meant that untrained ex-farmers frequently had to operate complex equipment, resulting in poor production and accidents.

> "The war had a huge impact on the economies of the three countries."[29]
>
> —Military historian Prit Buttar.

Furthermore, Stalin's focus on heavy industry meant that there were fewer regional facilities making the kinds of products needed for everyday life, such as farming and cooking implements. Importing these from elsewhere in the Soviet Union proved to be cumbersome and inefficient, so the people of the Baltic region suffered serious shortages of nearly everything—a situation that became the norm as the Soviet era wore on.

Another problem was Stalin's insistence on wildly unrealistic quotas designed to drive production rapidly forward. For example, the first Five-Year Plan demanded a 200 percent increase in iron production and a 335 percent increase in electrical power over previous figures. Managers and workers who could not meet these goals received punishments ranging from being denied food to being imprisoned or even, in some extreme cases, executed.

Desperate to meet unrealistic quotas, factory managers often inflated figures to make it seem that goals had been met. The rush to meet these quotas led to a wealth of other problems as well, such as increases in work related accidents. Shoddy manufacturing was another problem. Stories abounded about low-quality goods coming from the Baltics, from inferior steel to improperly sealed rubber raincoats that, once folded, could not be unfolded without breaking.

Famine

Shoddy products were a problem but not nearly as serious as the catastrophic food shortages and widespread famines that occurred in the Baltic nations, especially throughout the 1920s and 1930s. It is not known how many people in the Baltics died of starvation during the Soviet years, but one estimate puts the Soviet-wide figure at 5 million during a single famine in 1933.

There were several reasons for this string of deadly shortages. Naturally occurring droughts were partly to blame. Also, the thousands of

Red Army troops stationed in the Baltics required huge amounts of food. And the collective system of farming was not producing as much as predicted. Furthermore, the Soviet distribution system deprived the Baltics of food staples and instead sent them elsewhere, because Stalin considered those areas more important to the nation's economy. Virtually all of the food produced in the Baltic nations was exported east to other parts of the Soviet Union. Lithuanian, Latvian, and Estonian farms were not allowed to keep any food for themselves until quotas for export had been met. Since production was generally low, local farmers often could not keep any at all.

This had a tragic effect on daily life in the Baltics, both in the cities and the countryside. Simply put, there was never enough food. People sometimes tried to hide grain, but this was risky. If discovered by the authorities, the food was confiscated and the people responsible were severely punished. Journalist Ryszard Kapuscinski once described a scene he witnessed on numerous occasions: "In villages lying along railroad lines, peasants would rush forward toward the tracks whenever a train

Families wait in line for bread in Latvia in 1934. Food shortages followed by famine killed millions of people in the Baltics during the 1920s and 1930s.

was approaching. They would fall to their knees, raise their arms in supplication, cry out: 'Bread! Bread!' The train crews were instructed to shut the windows, draw the curtains."[30]

Mismanagement and other faults of collectivization meant that the vast majority of people in the Baltics viewed communism with anger and fear. First and foremost, they were terrified by the prospect of famine. But there were other reasons to hate collectivization. One was the loss of individual control: Joining a collective or a factory workforce was not voluntary, and people resented being forced to do so. Also, life on collective farms was harsh and the working conditions in factories brutal. And it soon became clear that there was little chance of Baltic workers and farmers keeping the things they grew or made, much less having access to items from outside the region.

As a result, small-scale revolts were common during the early years of collectivization. Arson, vandalism, attacks on party officials, and the destruction of crops that would otherwise be shipped far from the Baltics were almost commonplace. However, as the decades rolled on, the people of the Baltics became somewhat accustomed to their way of life, and that—combined with governmental repression—meant that violent action grew less intense over time.

Inequality Even in Times of Abundance

The people of the Baltics grew resigned to a diminished way of life, including stark gaps between socioeconomic classes. Although communism had promised to make everyone equal, government employees and Communist Party members enjoyed special privileges such as cars, spacious apartments, household appliances, and sufficient amounts of food. The average Baltic citizen was not as fortunate, however. It has been estimated, for example, that in the early 1960s urban Latvian families consumed 30 to 50 percent less meat, eggs, and dairy than before World War II. The figures were even higher in rural areas.

Meat was an especially precious commodity for ordinary citizens. If there were reports that it was available, people routinely traveled long distances in order to acquire it and other everyday items, like butter or cigarettes. Periodically, the Soviets imposed a rationing system, in which

Baltic citizens were allowed only a certain amount of food for a given period. This gave rise to a lively black market, in which people illegally sold or traded items for things they needed.

And even when food or goods were available, prices were generally beyond the reach of most people. For example, in 1958 the average annual wage for a farmer in the Baltics was about 68.6 rubles plus about 990 pounds (450 kg) of grain. To put that in perspective, 1 pound (454 g) of sausage cost about 2.8 rubles, a man's sweater cost 20 rubles, and a motorcycle was 980 rubles.

Improvements

Despite the obvious shortcomings, the economic situation in the Baltics was not completely dire. The mid- to late 1940s were the worst of the famine years, but afterward improved methods of farming slowly raised the region's agricultural output. By the early 1950s, for example, grain production finally reached prewar levels again. And as agriculture improved in the Baltics, so did manufacturing. This was particularly true after the 1950s, when Nikita Khrushchev opened up new trade opportunities in the West for Baltic-made electronics and other goods.

As a result, throughout the 1950s, 1960s, and 1970s, the Baltic nations were relatively well off compared to other regions of the Soviet Union. Lieven comments, "For what it was worth, relatively high food production [and] mass demand . . . for the products of their industries, together with their more prosperous and hard-working traditions, helped to give the Baltic States the highest quality of life in the Soviet Union."[31]

The Transition Begins

Throughout the 1970s and 1980s, the Baltic nations continued to enjoy a modest but relatively prosperous economy. Then, as elsewhere in the Soviet Union, the situation improved slowly as Mikhail Gorbachev initiated his reforms. Under these new policies, collectivization was slowly dismantled and replaced by a capitalist system.

At first, Gorbachev's reforms improved conditions in the Baltics, reviving the relatively sluggish economies of all the Baltic States. Foreign investment began to flow into the area. Private businesses such as restaurants

The State of Estonia's Economy

In a look back at the Estonian economic picture at the end of 2013, the nation's minister of finance, Jürgen Ligi, stated that as a whole he considered the year to be one of continued strong growth for Estonia. He commented that wages for workers were high and that "the economy and welfare are currently much better: the volume of deposits is higher, the overall loans burden is smaller, price growth has decelerated significantly. . . . Even the budget balance is better than during the boom years, when we saw a significant-seeming surplus, whereas a major deficit was lurking in the shadows. At the moment, the budget is structurally better balanced."

Quoted in Baltic Course, "Ligi: Estonia's Economy in Robust Health," December 27, 2013. www.baltic-course.com.

and shops sprang up on the streets of Baltic towns and cities, boosting local economies and improving the everyday lives of people. Other kinds of small private businesses were also allowed to operate, such as markets in which artisans and farmers could sell homemade or homegrown goods. Baltic citizens had the opportunity to start many other businesses as well. Reporter William J. Eaton noted in 1987, "Officials in Latvia have approved the establishment of a private dating service, a salon for pets and horse-drawn carriage rides through the old part of Riga."[32]

But Gorbachev was not able to fully stabilize the economy, and this was a major factor in the collapse of the Soviet Union in the late 1980s and early 1990s. Economic leaders of the Baltic countries were in many ways prepared for this. Lithuania, Latvia, and Estonia had been moving their financial structures toward a free-market system more rapidly than other parts of the USSR. Business journalist Heidi Brown writes about the Baltics, "They knew it was a priceless opportunity; they were small and nimble and situated right in the heart of Europe—able to communicate with investors from Western and Central Europe and, eventually, Russia."[33]

The Baltic Tiger

This new economic vigor represented a dramatic change for the Baltics—and not all of it was positive. In the years following independence, the transition from collectivization to private ownership created many problems. Corruption, misuse of power, and bribery were among those problems. One prominent example involved Latvia's major public energy company, Latvenergo. Top officials in this agency were convicted of taking advantage of the confusion caused by changes in the nation's economy to make illegal money transfers, transactions, and investments. However, such cases have been relatively rare, and overall the Baltic economies have functioned with little scandal.

More significantly, the region's overall economy has steadily improved, thanks to alliances with the West. One milestone in this process was reached in 2004, when all three nations joined the European Union

A butcher shows customers various cuts of meat at a market in the Lithuanian capital of Vilnius in 1990. Foreign investment gave a boost to businesses in the Baltic States around this time.

(EU), an organization that fosters mutual economic aid and growth on the European continent. Membership in the EU signifies that a country has reached a high level of economic stability and influence.

In the years since 2004, the overall Baltic economy improved, creating a boom nick-named the "Baltic Tiger." This boom had a profound impact on ordinary people in the region in areas such as increased job oppor-tunities, ranging from high-level professional positions to blue-collar employment. Some-times these jobs were overseas, but others were available in the Baltics. In many cases local jobs were supplied by foreign businesses such as Microsoft, McDonald's, Hertz, and the drug powerhouse Pfizer, all of which set up branches and joint ventures in the region.

> "They knew it was a priceless opportunity; they were small and nimble and situated right in the heart of Europe."[33]
>
> —Business journalist Heidi Brown.

The 2008–2009 global recession was a serious setback in the Baltics (as it was for countries around the world). The restrictions of the eco-nomic meltdown forced such measures as tightened national budgets and increased numbers of people leaving the region to find work in other countries. However, the economy of the Baltics has made steady improve-ments since the crisis.

Overall, the switch from communism to a free-market economy and the resulting economic alliances with the West profoundly changed life in the Baltics. If nothing else, the change gave the people of the Baltics greater access to consumer products and a wide range of outside cultural sources, such as music, film, and television. More than one observer has commented that independence—and with it a new economic order—changed life in the Baltics from black and white to color.

CHAPTER FOUR

Daily Life in the Baltics

Overall, daily life in the Baltics during the Soviet occupation was dominated by restriction, fear, and drabness. There were small pleasures, however, that gave life a distinctive flavor—celebrating a birthday, perhaps, by eating *klingeris*, a traditional Latvian bread with dried fruits and decorations made of flowers.

But such pleasant aspects of life were scarce. For ordinary people and even loyal officials, nearly every aspect of life was dominated by the suppression of perceived anti-Soviet behavior. Officials in Moscow were obsessed with rooting out "enemies of the people"—a category that included dissidents, criminals, former landowners, and academics. Anyone with even a slight foreign connection was deemed untrustworthy; this included such unlikely targets as stamp collectors who corresponded with people in other countries.

In large part the government rooted out alleged dissent by building a network of amateur spies drawn from ordinary Baltic citizens. These people were instructed to report suspected dissidents—even if those suspects were their friends, neighbors, or family members.

Because no one knew who might be willing to report on a suspect, everyday people in the Baltics feared saying anything, even in private, that might be taken as subversive. Something as simple as an overheard anti-Soviet joke was enough to invite a midnight raid and arrest by the NKVD, the much-feared Soviet secret police. And Baltic citizens knew better than to even express curiosity. Andrejs Plakans writes, "Friends and colleagues simply disappeared, and people quickly learned that it was dangerous to ask too many questions."[34]

The Gulags

Following arrest, suspects typically underwent interrogation and in some cases were tortured. Some convicted dissidents were executed, but far more common was imprisonment or deportation to labor camps called gulags. Gulag prisoners were responsible for the construction of projects such as canals, railroad lines, hydroelectric stations, roads, and manufacturing plants.

There were several hundred such camps scattered throughout distant, bleak regions of the Soviet Union. Officially, they were known as corrective labor camps, where subversives and criminals were reeducated to become part of the Soviet system. The Soviet regime insisted that the camps were benign. A party-sponsored book describing life in Estonia, for instance, asserted that the camps were for "the education of all workers in the spirit of Soviet patriotism and proletarian [working class] internationalism."[35]

> "Friends and colleagues simply disappeared, and people quickly learned that it was dangerous to ask too many questions."[34]
>
> —Historian Andrejs Plakans.

Deprivation and Death

Estimates vary widely on the total number of Baltic people sent to the gulags during the peak years of their operation, between 1929 and 1953—but even conservative estimates are staggering. Between 1944 and 1955 an estimated half million people were deported from the Baltics—roughly 124,000 from Estonia, 136,000 from Latvia, and 245,000 from Lithuania. The worst single example was a campaign in the spring of 1949, when an estimated 90,000 Baltic citizens were deported east. It has been reported that roughly three-quarters of them were women and children under the age of sixteen; many others were elderly, seriously ill, or disabled.

Many people from the Baltic region did not even reach their destinations. Already exhausted by months of imprisonment, interrogation, hunger, and beatings, they were forced to endure long journeys in unheated railroad boxcars on the way to the camps. Ryszard Kapuscinski

Prisoners pull a heavy load in a snow-covered Siberian gulag. Hundreds of thousands of Baltic residents were sent to Soviet gulags, where many thousands perished.

writes, "They faced weeks of torment in crowded cattle cars, in filth, [in] the delirium of thirst (for they weren't given anything to drink). They did not know where they were going or what awaited them at the end of the journey."[36]

Prisoners who did reach the camps faced similarly brutal conditions. The work was punishing and the living conditions cruel: meager food rations, clothing unsuitable for harsh winters, overcrowding, poorly insulated housing, bad or nonexistent hygiene facilities, physical and sexual abuse, and inadequate health care. The percentage of Baltic prisoners who died in the camps is uncertain, but an estimated 1 million to 1.5 million people from across the Soviet Union died in the gulags.

Censorship

Deportation to the gulags was an extreme example of the difficulties of life in the Baltics. Far more common were the hardships and humiliations of daily existence, including the suppression of ethnic traditions and religious observances. Traditionally, Estonia and parts of Latvia were primarily Lutheran, and Lithuania and a portion of Latvia were heavily Catholic. The Soviets banned these and other religions; they closed churches and arrested and imprisoned priests.

Another example of suppression in daily life was the heavy censorship of news from both internal and external sources. Gendrik Vartanyan, a factory supervisor, recalled, "Whatever that was written in the newspaper had to be in favor of the Soviet Union. . . . They could not write about anything bad that was going on at the time because the belief was that under Communist rule, nothing goes wrong."[37]

While censorship existed in the USSR as a whole, it was especially prominent in the Baltics because of the region's proximity to Western Europe. Since Baltic citizens were able to receive foreign radio and television broadcasts, they had a better grasp of what life in the West, with its relative freedom and affluence, could be like. Defying the government, people in the Baltics listened in secret and kept the spirit of dissent alive more than in other Soviet states. The Soviet government angrily denounced this. Writing in 1987, as the pro-independence movement gained momentum, *New York Times* reporter Bill Keller noted:

> The Soviet press has mounted an unusually bitter attack on Western radio stations for their role in publicizing nationalist demonstrations Sunday in the Soviet Baltic republics.
>
> In a weeklong stream of press and television reports, Soviet officials have accused "Western radio voices" beamed into the three republics—Lithuania, Latvia and Estonia—of instigating the demonstrations. The officials called the broadcasts a direct interference in the Soviet Union's domestic affairs.[38]

Education

Yet another striking example of Soviet oppression was the way in which the government controlled the education of young people in the Baltics. The educational system was free, but had a huge drawback: Students

Vacations for Some

The restrictions on movement, housing, food allotment, and other aspects of daily life in the Baltics had a negative impact on the vast majority of people there, but for a small minority—senior Communist Party officials—life was good. Loyalty to the party led to a wide variety of rewards such as private cars, summer homes, and plum work assignments. Another coveted privilege was an annual vacation at one of the many plush resorts on the Baltic Sea. Gunta Uspele, an administrator at a popular Soviet-era resort that is now under private ownership and open to the public, comments, "People from Russia came here as if they were really going abroad. Latvia seemed more like a part of Europe and people in the USSR thought of coming to Latvia like coming to France or Italy."

Quoted in Baltic Features, "Latvia's Soviet Holiday Heaven Finds a New Place in the Sun," August 17, 2009. http://balticfeatures.wordpress.com.

learned only one viewpoint. Specifically, history and social studies books were written to cast communism in a positive light. Stalin was portrayed as a noble savior, and his picture appeared in every classroom.

The Soviets repressed the use of native languages as well. Each Baltic nation had its own distinctive tongue. Latvian and Lithuanian were somewhat related to German and the Romance languages (such as Italian and French). Estonian, meanwhile, was more closely related to Finnish. During the Soviet years, classes in Russian—the official language—were officially optional. In practice, however, Russian was the only language taught in schools. Knowledge of Russian was also important elsewhere in everyday life in the Baltics, since it was the only language used in official matters. And it was essential for any student who aspired to higher study or a professional career, since it was the only language used in those environments.

Outside of school, students were expected to join the Baltic branches of organizations designed to teach young people how to be good Soviet citizens. Even after the worst practices ended with Stalin's death in 1953, young people in the Baltics were still shaped by Soviet policies and practices. It was the only life they knew. Eva Tarm, an Estonian born in 1958, comments:

> When I was growing up . . . no-one was seized at night, and there were no mass arrests; but . . . Soviet life was like a saw which cut everything down to one level, or a tailor who forced everyone to wear a grey overcoat. . . . It was like being in prison—either people found underhand ways of evading the system, or they developed hobbies which were really just substitutes for life outside the walls.[39]

Work

Adults in the Baltics experienced a similar degree of control and regulation. Under the Soviet system everyone was guaranteed a job. But people were often assigned unrewarding and unsatisfying work for which they had no experience. For example, a university professor might be assigned to menial labor in a factory or on a farm. The most prestigious and well-paying positions in management and government went to loyal Communist Party members.

Wages for most workers were low. And if harvests were bad or manufacturing production was less than expected, collective farms and factories paid workers only a tiny percentage of their already meager wages. As a result, most people in the Baltics were chronically short of money. They often had to supplement their incomes in unofficial ways, such as moonlighting as carpenters or plumbers or selling vegetables grown in private gardens.

The promise of full employment led to the creation of jobs just for the sake of having them; often this meant that several people carried out a job that could easily have been done with fewer workers. A joking

"Soviet life was like a saw which cut everything down to one level, or a tailor who forced everyone to wear a grey overcoat."[39]

—Estonian native Eva Tarm.

comment often heard in the Baltics during the Soviet years summed up the overall work environment: "We pretend to work, and they pretend to pay us."[40] Furthermore, the knowledge that their jobs were safe invited inefficiency and laziness—after all, there was little incentive for people to work hard if they knew they always had a job no matter how well or poorly they did it.

Housing

The housing situation was another way in which Soviet occupiers controlled daily life. Housing was especially critical in the region because World War II had destroyed much of the existing housing in the Baltics. At the end of the war in 1945, the region desperately needed new apartment buildings. As a result, hastily built high-rises were soon ringing the region's cities for miles in every direction. They were mass-produced; most of the construction took place in concrete factories, and parts were trucked to the building sites. This cookie-cutter approach resulted in buildings that were dreary, monolithic, and shoddy. The apartments within them were typically cramped. Several families were often forced to share apartments, so an entire family might live in a single room. Nonetheless, an apartment was a luxury for the millions of people who moved from rural areas and had only known life in basic farmhouses, which typically were small and had few modern amenities.

"We pretend to work, and they pretend to pay us."[40]

—Soviet workers' joke.

Adding to the dreariness of Soviet-era architecture, the facades of public buildings reflected the government's ideal of "socialist realism"— that is, art that glorified the goals of communism at the expense of beauty. Historian Anne Applebaum writes, "By the early 1950s, all the gray, war-damaged [towns and buildings of the Baltics] were patrolled by the same kinds of unsmiling policemen, designed by the same socialist realist architects, and draped with the same kinds of propaganda posters."[41] The government controlled how apartments were allotted. It also restricted relocation from one area of the Baltics to another, or to another part of the USSR. Passports and other official documents, such as work orders,

Huge, dreary apartment complexes similar to this one in Latvia were built during the Soviet era. Several families were often forced to share an apartment, with whole families living in a single cramped room.

were mandatory, and people frequently had to wait months or even years before a relocation request was approved.

The government controlled movement for several reasons. One was to direct people to urban centers as the region's need for industrialization (and thus for workers) increased. But there was another reason for restricting movement: people who protested policies or otherwise angered Soviet authorities could be banished to undesirable locations, such as remote rural areas. Sometimes an entire village suffered punishment for infractions such as organizing a protest against food shortages. This punishment could essentially cut the offending village off from any contact with the outside world and could be extremely harsh. Kapuscinski writes, "The authorities closed village shops, schools, and medical clinics. Peasants were not allowed to leave their villages, were prevented from entering the towns. Signs were placed along the roads near the entrances to villages considered mutinous: STOPPING HERE IS FORBIDDEN, SPEAKING WITH ANYONE IS FORBIDDEN!"[42]

Food Shortages

Still another prominent example of the restrictions of everyday life in the Baltics concerned food and other basic goods. The years of collectivization had created a chaotic distribution system for goods imported from outside the region, and locally made goods and food products were often unavailable. This resulted in chronic shortages of everything from luxury items to basic necessities.

Because of this, the government sometimes was forced to impose rationing. Even without rationing, food shortages were a tedious and frustrating part of daily life. Historians Romuald Misiunas and Rein Taagepera comment, "To buy food, one had to stand in three or four separate waiting lines, and then take the streetcar to separate bakery and vegetable stores, only to find some of them closed for lunch."[43]

Even if a store was open, a person might stand in a line for hours with no guarantee once he or she reached the front of the line that supplies would still be available. So the people of the Baltics often were forced to fend for themselves as best they could, trading on the black market or tending private gardens.

The chronic shortage of goods meant that people in the Baltics had to be on constant lookout for what was available at a given moment. Word of mouth was often how people found out about something on sale. For example, word might spread that a certain shop had a shipment of bananas or toothpaste. People would rush there to stand in line. One observer likened life in this regard to a year-round Christmas rush. Women (and in some cases men) routinely carried bags with them so that they could stop on the spur of the moment and wait in line if they encountered an opportunity. Sometimes people simply saw lines and joined them, buying whatever was available in case they might need it in the future.

Drinking

Even in times of extreme shortages, one item was always cheap and readily available: alcohol—especially vodka, the national drink. Alcohol could relieve the multiple stresses of everyday life, but it also created a serious social problem: during the Soviet era the Baltics had one of the highest

A Midnight Visit from the Secret Police

Journalist Ryszard Kapuscinski here vividly describes a typical arrest of a dissident by the Soviet Union's much-feared secret police:

> The method here is surprise. The person is asleep, and suddenly shouts awake him, he sees above him the fierce faces of soldiers and of the [secret police]; they pull him out of bed, shove him with rifle butts, and command him to leave the house. They order that weapons be handed over, which of course no one possesses anyway. The whole time they spew vile obscenities. . . . They turn the whole house upside down, and they take the greatest delight in this. . . . The house is left empty, for they take the entire family—grandparents, children, everyone.

Ryszard Kapuscinski, *Imperium*. New York: Vintage, 1995, p. 10.

percentages of alcoholism in the world. A 1970 study showed that the Baltics consumed 50 percent more alcohol per capita than the average in the rest of the USSR (which in turn was among the top nations of the world in alcohol consumption).

Suicide rates in the Baltics were also among the highest in the world, a situation aggravated, at least in part, by the combination of alcoholism and the stress of daily life. Lieven notes: "Anyone who has visited the Baltics will know of sad middle-aged people, whose families excuse their drinking by pointing to the hopelessness and the endless petty humiliations of Soviet rule."[44]

Ethnic Revival and Ethnic Tensions

These endless humiliations—along with the far more serious issues of suppression of free speech and isolation from the outside world—shaped life in the Baltic States during Soviet rule. But the collapse of the Soviet Union and independence for the Baltics brought an end to many of the old restrictions and resulted in countless ways in which daily life was enriched.

For one thing, the use of native languages immediately saw a strong revival, both as classes in schools and in daily life. For example, Latvia passed the Latvian Language Law in 1989, and in 1991 Latvian became the official state language. Today national and regional commissions in Latvia continue to promote its use. On the other hand, the increased use of ethnic languages and other aspects of Baltic culture have created tensions between Baltic natives and Russians. During the Soviet era many Russians were relocated to the Baltic countries and have since raised families there. But Russians living in the Baltic countries face hurdles that others do not face.

As part of the process of reviving native culture in Estonia, after independence that nation denied citizenship to ethnic Russians, who make up about one-quarter of the population, thus denying them rights such as the right to vote. Today knowledge of the Estonian language remains a requirement for citizenship. Furthermore, ethnic Russians living in Estonia have had difficulty finding good jobs. Ethnic Russians remain concerned about their status as second-class citizens who are denied, to a large degree, equal rights and the chance for a good life.

The old Soviet regime is now a distant memory for older people in the Baltics. For younger people born after the Soviet Union's collapse, the Soviet occupation exists only as a chapter in a history book. In many ways the region has rebuilt itself remarkably well since the Soviet occupation. But in many ways serious challenges lie ahead for Lithuania, Latvia, and Estonia.

CHAPTER FIVE

The Challenges Ahead

The end of Soviet communism was an exhilarating period for the people of the Baltics, when freedom—almost unthinkable for a long time—became reality. During the decades of Soviet rule, it seemed that the independence of Baltic politics and cultures were doomed to be submerged within the monolithic Soviet Union. But all that changed and with the changes came challenges that remain for the future of the region. Among these were significant shifts in the political, economic, and social structures of each of the Baltic States.

The Future of Baltic Politics

The internal political structure of each of the Baltic nations, based on a Western-style constitutional democratic parliamentary system, is likely to remain in place in the future. However, the political situation can be volatile when circumstances trigger rapid change. One striking example of this came late in 2013, when a supermarket roof collapsed in the Latvian capital of Riga, killing fifty-four people and touching off a dramatic ripple effect. The nation's prime minister, Valdis Dombrovskis, was a popular politician who was widely credited with bringing Latvia back from near bankruptcy. He had been expected to sail through an easy reelection in 2014. But in the wake of the tragedy he resigned, accepting responsibility amid accusations that authorities had turned a blind eye to lax building standards. After his resignation Dombrovskis's coalition government collapsed, and political chaos ensued as the nation scrambled to find a replacement.

In international politics, there are also serious issues at hand for the three Baltic nations. Notably, in 2014, Russia annexed Crimea, an autonomous Black Sea republic of southern Ukraine, after the Russian-majority region voted overwhelmingly to leave Ukraine and join Moscow. Lithuania, Latvia, and Estonia—which also have large ethnic Russian populations—worried about what an emboldened, aggressive Russia might mean for them. Russia had been showing signs of increased aggression for a while. For example, in 2013 Russia held unusually large-scale military exercises along the borders of Poland, Latvia, and Lithuania. As a result, even after years of independence, many Baltic citizens still fear a threat to peace and security. Polls in Latvia indicate that a significant majority of ethnic Latvians see Russia as just such a threat, and anti-Russian protest demonstrations have periodically taken place in the region. Nils Muiznieks, head of the Latvian Centre for Human Rights and Ethnic Studies in Riga, comments, "There is a feeling that we only won it [independence] because Russia was weak. Russia always was scary, it still is scary, and it always will be scary."[45]

> "Russia always was scary, it still is scary, and it always will be scary."[45]
>
> —Latvian human rights advocate Nils Muiznieks.

On the other hand, some observers dismiss the idea that Russia will prove to be a serious threat in the region or beyond. They argue that the Baltics, and Europe as a whole, are strong enough to withstand any aggressive move by Russia, such as the simulated air assault on Swedish military installations carried out by Russian aircraft in 2013. International policy expert Parag Khanna notes, "Every few years there is talk of a 'new iron curtain,' but Europe always knocks it down with its velvet glove."[46]

Reaching Out

While remaining wary of such possible outside threats, the governments of the Baltic nations continue to make efforts to reach out politically to other nations. For example, the governments of the Baltics are helping the African nations of Somalia and Ethiopia to bolster their security capabilities. Also, the three Baltic States are taking on increasingly important roles in European politics. One example of this is that all three nations play key roles in lobbying for North Atlantic Treaty Organization (NATO) membership for Georgia and other former Soviet states. Also, Estonia is assisting Georgia in implementing a variety of reforms and in creating defenses against cyberattacks. Latvia is helping enact reform efforts within Moldova's justice system. And

Reflecting on Twenty Years of Freedom

In 2010, on the twentieth anniversary of independence for the Baltics, Paul Goble, a senior member of the US Department of State and an expert on the region, reflected on the dramatic changes in the Baltics since the previous era. Before independence, he noted, the governments of Latvia, Lithuania, and Estonia were not recognized by any foreign nations, and their citizens lived under an economic and political system "that combined the worst forms of economic life with an arbitrary, authoritarian and often brutal political regime, one that openly celebrated the supremacy of the occupiers over the occupied." Goble continued:

> What is the case today? The Soviet troops are gone along with the Soviet Union; the Communists are out of office, completely discredited even if their crimes have not yet been adequately judged; the three Baltic countries are members of the United Nations, recognized by the overwhelming majority of the world's countries, and full partners of both the European Union and NATO; and Estonians, Latvians and Lithuanians live under conditions of democracy and free markets, enjoying all the advantages of both.

Quoted in *Economist*, "20 Years of Baltic Independence: Home but Not Dry," August 30, 2011. www.economist.com.

Lithuania is now the home of an institution of higher learning, the European Humanities University, which the repressive government of Belarus expelled in 2004.

The efforts of the Baltic nations to reach out in this way are summarized in a statement by Urmas Paet, Maris Riekstins, and Vygaudas Usackas, seasoned foreign affairs officials in Estonia, Latvia, and Lithuania, respectively:

> As members of the EU, NATO, OSCE [Organization for Security and Co-operation in Europe] and the United Nations, we have applied the spirit and principles of the Baltic Way when assisting the democratization process in neighboring countries to the East. Today, we participate in peacekeeping operations and send our experts to share our experience in establishing a civil society, promoting human rights, and fostering the development of non-governmental organizations.[47]

Future Challenges for the Baltic Economy

Politics is always closely allied with economics, and the question of maintaining and expanding the economies of the three Baltic nations will provide its own challenges for the future. The process of recovering from the global 2008–2009 economic meltdown has been slow in the Baltics, but it has been faster than in other parts of Europe.

"Every few years there is talk of a 'new iron curtain,' but Europe always knocks it down with its velvet glove."[46]

—International policy expert Parag Khanna.

One measure is that in 2013 the World Bank classified all three Baltic States as "high-income" economies, meaning that they are some of the top nations in the world as measured by their GNPs. (GNP, or gross national product, is a measure of a nation's products and services.) Foreign policy expert Damon Wilson commented in 2013, "Against a backdrop of economic stagnation and the Eurozone crisis, the Baltic [states] represent a healthy exception—a bright spot for growth, innovation, and

High-rise buildings in the capital of Tallinn illustrate the new Estonia. Like the other Baltic nations, Estonia faces many political and economic challenges as it modernizes.

competitiveness in Europe. They boast among the most open economies in Europe. . . . These nations now are among the most innovative, entrepreneurial, and technologically advanced economies in Europe."[48]

But maintaining that growth will be a challenge for the future. One example involves Latvia's entry as the eighteenth member of the Eurozone in 2013, an occasion marked by a massive fireworks display and tolling bells in Riga, the nation's capital. (Eurozone nations are those countries within the EU that use the euro as their currency. The total number of EU member nations is twenty-eight, but ten have so far chosen to keep their own currencies.)

The switch to the euro was not completely smooth. Within Latvia it caused considerable controversy, with polls indicating that more than

> "Against a backdrop of economic stagnation and the Eurozone crisis, the Baltic [states] represent a healthy exception—a bright spot for growth, innovation, and competitiveness in Europe."[48]
>
> —Foreign policy expert Damon Wilson.

half of the citizens opposed it. Chief among their concerns was the fear that Latvia would be forced to bail out other Eurozone nations, notably Spain and Greece, which experienced deep economic woes.

However, Latvia was able to avoid this fate. In fact, it had recovered from the 2008 recession more quickly than most of the EU, including economic powerhouses such as Germany. In large part this was because the Latvian government imposed strict austerity measures that sharply curbed expenditures. Adopting the euro was a significant symbol of this economic rebound, putting the country on a more equal footing with the major European nations. Many observers hailed the occasion as a major step forward. European Commission president José Manuel Barroso stated:

> This is a major event, not only for Latvia, but for the euro area itself. . . . For Latvia, it is the result of impressive efforts and the unwavering determination of the authorities and the Latvian people. Thanks to these efforts, undertaken in the aftermath of a deep economic crisis, Latvia will enter the euro area stronger than ever, sending an encouraging message to other countries undergoing a difficult economic adjustment.[49]

The EU's economic and monetary affairs commissioner, Olli Rehn, echoed this sentiment in an address to the people of Latvia. Rehn commented, "Joining the euro marks the completion of Latvia's journey back to the political and economic heart of our continent, and that is something for all of us to celebrate. Your efforts have paid off, and your country's strong economic recovery offers a clear message of encouragement to other European countries undergoing a difficult economic adjustment."[50]

Ethnic Discrimination and the Language Issue

Social conditions in the Baltics pose still more challenges for the region's future. One of the most important of these is the issue of human rights for ethnic minorities. The issue evokes passionate emotions, pitting people who want to protect their heritage and erase a difficult past against a minority that is demanding equal rights and a fair chance for a good life.

Although discrimination in the Baltics is, of course, not limited only to ethnic Russians, this group is the most affected. In particular, ethnic Russians throughout the Baltics continue to suffer disproportionately high unemployment and an inability to become naturalized citizens, which in turn denies them the right to vote. (There is a partial exception to this: Noncitizens in Estonia can vote in local elections.) Many ethnic natives and ethnic Russians no doubt coexist perfectly well, intermingling and in some cases intermarrying. However, there is clear evidence that ethnic Russians still suffer from discrimination.

Latvia and its picturesque capital, Riga (shown), celebrated the country's entry into the Eurozone in 2013. Strong government action helped Latvia recover quickly from the 2008 global recession.

Success Stories

According to historian Kevin O'Connor, the Baltic countries weathered the difficult first years of independence and entered the new millennium as the success stories of the former USSR, especially compared to other former Soviet states—and, he notes, they intend to stay successful. He adds:

> Whereas poverty and dictatorship have been the hallmarks of many of the new states that emerged from the rubble of the Soviet Union—one need only look at nearby Belarus, a country seemingly frozen in the Soviet past, to find a suitable European contrast—the Baltic countries are democratic and economically vigorous. . . .
>
> Lithuania, Latvia, and especially Estonia have in the fullest sense returned to Europe; the return to power of any party that frankly calls itself "communist" is as inconceivable as the prospect of willingly returning to the Russian orbit.

Kevin O'Connor, *The History of the Baltic States.* Westport, CT: Greenwood, 1993, pp. 196–97.

One problem that crystallizes this issue is the place of the Russian language in modern Baltic society. Many ethnic Russians argue that Russian should be adopted as a second official language. They argue that Russians in the Baltics are proud of their heritage and that putting Russian on an equal footing with existing official languages can help alleviate the pressures of second-class citizenship.

On the other hand, many ethnic natives passionately oppose the idea. In part this is because it invokes the days of Stalin-era occupation, when native languages were banned. And some activists feel that the movement is nothing more than an attempt by Russia to weaken the Baltic nations' independence and push them closer to Russia's sphere of influence. At the same time, some observers feel that there are simply more important issues at hand—that the controversy over language is only a distraction. Iveta Kažoka, a Latvian political analyst, comments, "Latvians should stop thinking of themselves in ethnic and language categories and together consider important questions about the development of the state."[51]

Illustrating the language issue was a nationwide referendum held in Latvia in 2012 on the idea of a constitutional amendment to include Russian as a second official language. The proposal was soundly defeated. Even if all of the country's ethnic Russians had been allowed to vote (they make up about one-third of the population), it would not have passed.

Some Latvians feel that the 2012 referendum should be seen as a positive way to continue the debate, by opening up discussions on how minority and majority groups can put their differences aside. Nil Ushakov, the mayor of the capital city of Riga, is an ethnic Russian who speaks Latvian. He told reporters, "Ethnic Latvians will be able more effectively and securely to develop and preserve their culture, language and other values if Russian-speaking Latvian residents are allies, not enemies."[52]

Crime

The language controversy is only one aspect of the issues facing minority groups in the Baltics. Another is the disproportionate amount of criminal activity in the region. In any culture the stress of being on the margins of society has a ripple effect, wherein troubles such as depression and poverty lead to problems such as disproportionate rates of substance abuse, HIV infection, and crime. The Baltics are no exception. These problems are far more frequent in ethnically Russian communities there than in the region as a whole.

For example, Estonia has the highest per capita drug-related death rate in the EU. Experts say that this is due almost completely to the widespread abuse of synthetic heroin within the country's Russian-speaking

Lithuania's capital, Vilnius (pictured), is a mixture of both old and new construction. Lithuania has made a strong global showing in meeting important environmental goals.

minority. Estonia's minister of the interior, Ken-Marti Vaher, acknowledges that his country's government has yet to deal adequately with the situation. However, he has pledged to make solving this ongoing tragedy an urgent concern for his government in the future. He remarks, "It is true that there are considerably more Russian speakers among injecting drug addicts. The reason could partially be the fact that injected drugs first spread to Estonia among the Russian-speaking population in the beginning of the '90s, when times were hard and social protection structures were not functioning. . . . This will remain a priority for the upcoming years."[53]

The Future of the Environment

Another challenge for the future of the Baltics is an ongoing concern over the effects of industry and growth on the environment. This issue dates back to the 1970s. At a time when more direct criticism of the government had to remain discreet, environmentalism served as an important "testing ground" for the limits of political activism in the Baltics. Today the situation has changed dramatically. Environmental activists and government authorities alike are able to openly address issues such as water purification, clean energy, radioactive waste sites, and pesticides. As a result, the Baltic nations have made impressive strides toward improving the quality of their environment.

For example, all of the nations perform well in the Yale and Columbia Environmental Performance Index, an annual compilation of how nations are faring in achieving environmental goals. Latvia's record is especially impressive. In the 2012 report, it was in second place out of 132 nations, topped only by Switzerland. Lithuania was ranked seventeenth and Estonia fifty-fourth.

Overall, the Baltic region has been significantly aided in its environmental efforts by the neighboring Scandinavian countries, which are understandably concerned with keeping the region healthy—especially the shared Baltic Sea. The Scandinavian nations have invested hundreds of millions of dollars in ecologically sound "green" enterprises in the Baltics, such as harmless methods of cleaning up oil spills and chemical dumping.

These and other efforts to improve the Baltic States' environmental practices are examples of how the Baltic nations continue to look to the West for inspiration and help. Daiva Semeniene, director of the Center for Environmental Policy in Vilnius, Lithuania, sums this up when she comments, "We're trying to reach not only the Scandinavian standard of living, but also its environmental standards, too."[54]

The Baltic nations have experienced huge changes in all facets of life. After years of repressive rule by the Soviets—and before that, hundreds of years of similar occupations by outside forces—the Baltic peoples now enjoy a relatively high degree of independence and prosperity. Many issues, from politics and the economy to ethnic tensions and the environment, will undoubtedly prove challenging but rewarding for the people of Latvia, Lithuania, and Estonia in the years ahead.

☭ SOURCE NOTES

Introduction: Inside Lithuania, Latvia, and Estonia

1. Sheila Fitzpatrick, "The Good Old Days," *London Review of Books*, October 9, 2003. www.lrb.co.uk.

2. Anne Applebaum, *Iron Curtain: The Crushing of Eastern Europe, 1944–1956*. New York: Random House, 2012, p. xxi.

3. Quoted in Royal Air Force Museum: National Cold War Exhibition, "Joseph Stalin," 2013. www.nationalcoldwarexhibition.org.

4. Anatol Lieven, *The Baltic Revolution: Estonia, Latvia, Lithuania and the Path to Independence*. New Haven, CT: Yale University Press, 1993, p. 82.

5. Archie Brown, "Reform, Coup and Collapse: The End of the Soviet State," BBC, February 17, 2011. www.bbc.co.uk.

6. Quoted in Adrian Bridge, "New Beat in the Baltic," *Sydney Morning Herald* (Australia), September 10, 2011. www.smh.com.au.

Chapter One: Controlling the Baltics

7. Andrejs Plakans, *A Concise History of the Baltic States*. Cambridge: Cambridge University Press, 2011, pp. xiii–xiv.

8. Kevin O'Connor, *The History of the Baltic States*. Westport, CT: Greenwood, 1993, pp. 115–16.

9. Quoted in Michael Wines, "A 'Forest Brother' Remembers a Life on the Run," *New York Times*, August 23, 2003. www.nytimes.com.

10. Plakans, *A Concise History of the Baltic States*, p. 344.

11. Quoted in Romuald J. Misiunas and Rein Taagepera, *The Baltic States: Years of Dependence, 1940–1990*. Berkeley: University of California Press, 1993, p. 27.

12. Quoted in Misiunas and Taagepera, *The Baltic States*, pp. 22–23.

13. Prit Buttar, *Between Giants: The Battle for the Baltics in World War II*. Oxford: Osprey, 2013, p. 103.

14. Quoted in Laurence Rees, *WWII Behind Closed Doors*. New York: Random House, 2004, p. 224.

15. Plakans, *A Concise History of the Baltic States*, pp. 340, 344.

16. Quoted in Michael Dobbs, *Six Months in 1945: From World War to Cold War*. New York: Knopf, 2012, p. 249.

Chapter Two: Politics in the Baltics

17. Quoted in Li Bennich-Björkman, "The Communist Past: Party Formation and Elites in the Baltic States," *Baltic Worlds*, February 12, 2010. http://balticworlds.com.

18. Quoted in Misiunas and Taagepera, *The Baltic States*, pp. 165–66.

19. Quoted in Jason MacLeod, "The Nonviolent Liberation of Latvia," *Change Agency*, January 2009. www.thechangeagency.org.

20. Quoted in Owen Matthews, "The New Scandinavians," *Newsweek*, June 28, 2008. www.newsweek.com.

21. Mark R. Beissinger, "Nationalism and the Collapse of Soviet Communism." *Contemporary European History*, 2009, http://www.princeton.edu/~mbeissin/beissinger.ceh.article.pdf.

22. Quoted in Esther B. Fein, "Baltic Independence Fronts Plead to U.N.," *New York Times*, May 15, 1989. www.nytimes.com.

23. Quoted in Rose Brady, "The Tanks Hesitated, Then Lurched Forward . . . ," *Businessweek*, January 27, 1991. www.businessweek.com.

24. Lievan, *The Baltic Revolution: Estonia, Latvia, Lithuania and the Path to Independence,* p. 131.

25. Plakans, *A Concise History of the Baltic States*, pp. 400–401.

26. O'Connor, *The History of the Baltic States*, p. 164.

Chapter Three: Economics in the Baltics

27. Quoted in History Learning Site, "Collectivisation of Agriculture in Russia." www.historylearningsite.co.uk.

28. Quoted in Daniel Humphrey, "Saving the Other/Rescuing the Self," *Invisible Culture*, 2003. www.rochester.edu.

29. Buttar, *Between Giants*, p. 321.

30. Ryszard Kapuscinski, *Imperium*. New York: Vintage, 1995, pp. 286–87.

31. Lieven, *The Baltic Revolution*, p. 98.

32. William J. Eaton, "New Entrepreneurs Rush to Supply Consumers in Estonia, Latvia," *Los Angeles Times*, May 10, 1987. http://articles.la times.com.

33. Heidi Brown, "The Baltics: Pampering Foreign Investors," *Forbes*, February 6, 2006. www.forbes.com.

Chapter 4: Daily Life in the Baltics

34. Plakans, *A Concise History of the Baltic States*, pp. 345–46.

35. Quoted in Misiunas and Taagepera, *The Baltic States*, p.80.

36. Kapuscinski, *Imperium*, p. 201.

37. Quoted in Nelli Ohanjanyan, "Life in the Soviet Union—Gendrik Vartanyan," Clark Humanities. www.clarkhumanities.org.

38. Bill Keller, "Russians Say Western Radio Instigated Baltic Protests," *New York Times*, August 25, 1987. www.nytimes.com.

39. Quoted in Lievan, *The Baltic Revolution*, p. 82.

40. Quoted in Paul F. deLespinasse, "One Way to Full Employment: Soviets Used Very Low Wages," *Albany (OR) Democrat-Herald*, October 23, 2001. http://democratherald.com.

41. Applebaum, *Iron Curtain*, p. xxv.

42. Kapuscinski, *Imperium*, pp. 286–87.

43. Misiunas and Taagepera, *The Baltic States*, p. 212.

44. Lieven, *The Baltic Revolution*, p. 98.

Chapter 5: The Challenges Ahead

45. Quoted in Peter Ford, "Russia Five Years After the Fall," *Christian Science Monitor*, June 2, 1997. www.csmonitor.com.

46. Parag Khanna, *The Second World: Empire and Influence in the New Global Order*. New York: Random House, 2008, p. 23.

47. Urmas Paet, Māris Riekstiņš, and Vygaudas Ušackas, "The Baltic Way," *Wall Street Journal*, October 26, 2009. http://online.wsj.com.

48. Damon Wilson, "The Baltic Way." *Atlantic Council*, August 28, 2013. www.atlanticcouncil.org.

49. Quoted in Carol J. Williams, "Latvia Joins Eurozone with New Year's Fanfare but Little Joy," *Los Angeles Times*, December 31, 2013. www.latimes.com.

50. Quoted in Aaron Eglitis, "Latvia Becomes 18th Euro-area Member Despite Lingering Animosity," *Vancouver (BC) Sun*, January 1, 2014. www.vancouversun.com.

51. Quoted in Aleks Tapinsh, "Russian Language Vote Shows Ethnic Split in Latvia," Reuters, February 17, 2012. http://in.reuters.com.

52. Quoted in Tapinsh, "Russian Language Vote Shows Ethnic Split in Latvia."

53. Quoted in Michael Amundsen, "Why Is 'China White' Killing Estonia's Russian Speakers?," *Christian Science Monitor*, October 16, 2013. www.csmonitor.com.

54. Quoted in Matthews, "The New Scandinavians."

Geography

- Size: Lithuania, 25,174 sq mi (65,200 sq km), Latvia 24,938 sq mi (64,589 sq km), Estonia 17,462 sq mi (45, 226 sq km)
- The Baltic Sea is 160,335 square miles (415,266 sq km); it is the largest body of brackish (part salt, part fresh) water in the world.
- Highest point of the three countries: Suur Munamägi ("Big Egg Mountain"), Estonia: 1,043 feet (317.9 m).

People and Society

- Literacy is nearly 100 percent in all three countries.
- Populations (2013 estimates):
    Estonia: 1,286,540
    Latvia: 2,013,400
    Lithuania: 2,955,986
- Percentages of native ethnic population:
    Estonia: 69 percent ethnic Estonians
    Lithuania: 84.1 percent ethnic Lithuanians
    Latvia: 62.1 percent ethnic Latvians
- Main religions:
    Estonia: Lutheran, Orthodox Christian
    Latvia: Lutheran, Catholic, Russian Orthodox
    Lithuania: Catholic
- Capital cities:
    Tallinn (Estonia)
    Riga (Latvia)
    Vilnius (Lithuania)

Government

- Formal names: Republic of Estonia, Republic of Latvia, Republic of Lithuania.

- All three countries achieved independence in 1991.
- All three countries are parliamentary republics.
- All three countries joined NATO and the EU in 2004.
- First female head of state in the Baltics: Vaira Vīķe-Freiberga, elected president of Latvia in 1999.

Economy

- Main agricultural products of the region: grain, potatoes, vegetables, livestock and dairy products, fish.
- Main manufacturing or service products of the region: electronics, wood and wood products, textiles, information technology, telecommunications.
- Currencies (as of 2013):
  Estonia: euro
  Latvia: lats
  Lithuania: litas
- Most oil, electricity, and other energy sources are imported.
- The region has high rankings in productivity among European countries.

Communications

- Sophisticated computer infrastructure, with high rankings in Internet upload and download speeds.
- The software for Skype was developed in Estonia.
- Number of Internet users (as of June 30, 2012):
  Estonia: 993,785
  Latvia: 1,570,925
  Lithuania: 2,293,508
- Number of Facebook users (as of December 31, 2013):
  Estonia: 501,680
  Latvia: 414,520
  Lithuania: 1,118,500

FOR FURTHER RESEARCH

Books

Noah Berlatsky, ed., *Stalin's Great Purge*. Farmington Hills, MI: Greenhaven, 2012.

Sylvia Engdahl, ed., *The Bolshevik Revolution*. Farmington Hills, MI: Greenhaven, 2013.

Kayla Morgan, *The Cold War*. Minneapolis, MN: Abdo, 2010.

Steven Otfinoski, *The Baltic Republics*. New York: Facts On File, 2004.

Jim Willis, *Daily Life Behind the Iron Curtain*. Westport, CT: Greenwood, 2013.

Websites

Baltic Review (http://baltic-review.com). A good source of current news about the nations bordering the Baltic Sea.

Hoover Institution, Baltic States—Historical Overview (www.hoover .org/library-and-archives/collections/east-europe/baltic-states/history). An excellent source of images, blogs, basic information, and more, maintained by the Hoover Institution at Stanford University.

History Learning Site, Cold War (www.historylearningsite.co.uk/cold war.htm). Detailed information on the East-West espionage and arms buildup of the Soviet era.

Gulag: Soviet Forced Labor Camps and the Struggle for Freedom (http://gulaghistory.org/nps). Fascinating but grim—a wealth of information on a site maintained by the Center for History and New Media at George Mason University.

History.com, Joseph Stalin (www.history.com/topics/joseph-stalin). Videos, transcribed speeches, biographical information, and more about the Soviet dictator.

INDEX

ABOUT THE AUTHOR

Adam Woog is the author of many books for children, teens, and adults. He also writes a column for the *Seattle Times* and is a preschool teacher. Woog lives with his wife in Seattle, Washington. They have an adult daughter.